I0797665

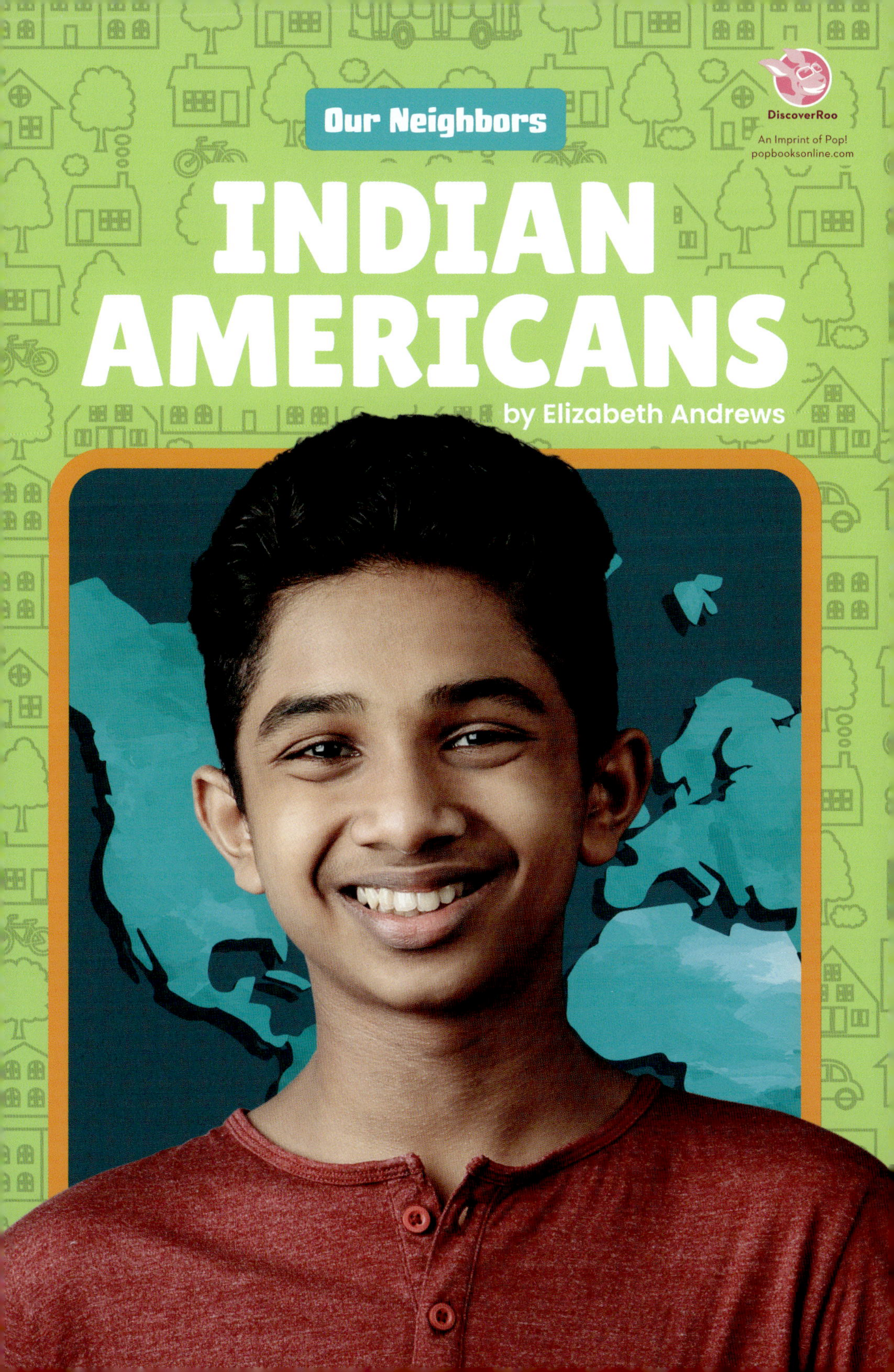

INDIAN AMERICANS

by Elizabeth Andrews

abdobooks.com

Published by Pop!, a division of ABDO, PO Box 398166, Minneapolis, Minnesota 55439.

Printed in the United States of America, North Mankato, Minnesota.

052021
092021

THIS BOOK CONTAINS RECYCLED MATERIALS

Cover Photos: Shutterstock Images

Interior Photos: Shutterstock Images, 1, 5, 11, 14–15, 18, 26–27; iStockphoto, 6, 8–9, 17, 23, 28–29; Barbara Walton/AP/Shutterstock, 12; Aman Sharma/AP/Shutterstock, 20 (top); Universal History Archive/UIG/Shutterstock, 20 (bottom); Saurabh Das/AP/Shutterstock, 21 (top); Ajit Kumar/AP/Shutterstock, 21 (bottom); London News Pictures/Shutterstock, 24

Editor: Tyler Gieseke
Series Designer: Laura Graphenteen

Library of Congress Control Number: 2020948836

Publisher's Cataloging-in-Publication Data

Names: Andrews, Elizabeth, author.

Title: Indian Americans / by Elizabeth Andrews

Description: Minneapolis, Minnesota : Pop!, 2022 | Series: Our neighbors | Includes online resources and index.

Identifiers: ISBN 9781098240035 (lib. bdg.) | ISBN 9781644945971 (pbk.) | ISBN 9781098240950 (ebook)

Subjects: LCSH: East Indian Americans--Juvenile literature. | Ethnicity--United States--Juvenile literature. | Neighbors--Juvenile literature. | Immigrants--United States--History--Juvenile literature.

Classification: DDC 973.004--dc23

WELCOME TO DiscoverRoo!

Pop open this book and you'll find QR codes loaded with information, so you can learn even more!

Scan this code* and others like it while you read, or visit the website below to make this book pop!

popbooksonline.com/indian-americans

*Scanning QR codes requires a web-enabled smart device with a QR code reader app and a camera.

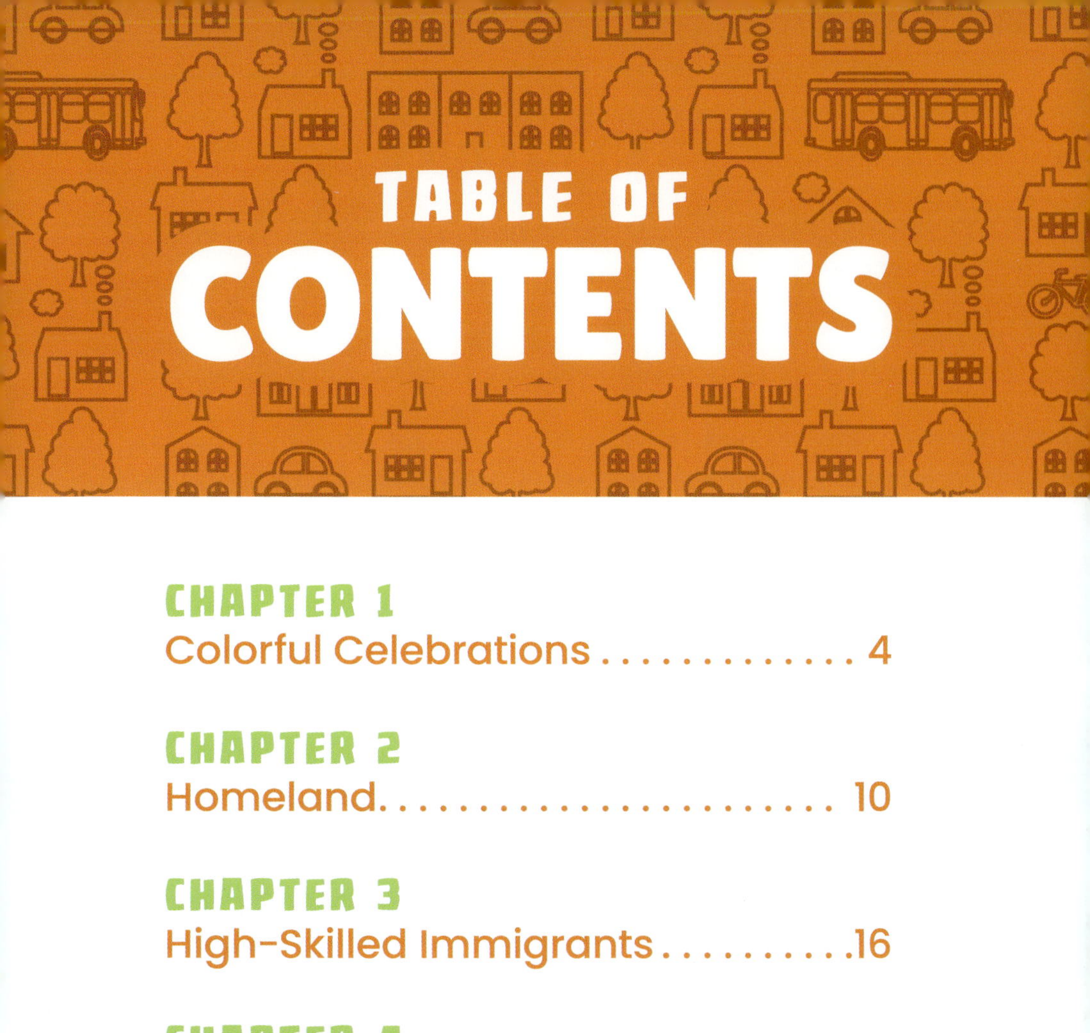

TABLE OF CONTENTS

COLORFUL CELEBRATIONS

Naveen woke up well rested and excited for the day ahead. He had spent yesterday cleaning with his parents and sister. Everything was tidy for the

WATCH A VIDEO HERE!

All kinds of fireworks are lit during Diwali.

celebrations. He had even laid out his new purple silk *kurta* before he went to bed. His mother and sister will be in their best *saris*.

The Diwali oil lamp is called a diya.

The sari is a garment made of elegant fabric that can be worn in 100 different ways on the body. It is India's oldest art form.

Today was the first day of *Diwali* celebrations. Diwali is the festival of lights. It **symbolizes** good defeating evil in the Hindu religion. Naveen and his family work together to light rows of colorful oil lamps. They decorate their home with flowers. His favorite part is watching his mother create the *rangoli* art on their entryway floor.

The family's cleaning and decorating has an even greater purpose. They want everything to be clean and welcoming. Soon, they will do a **ritual** to invite the goddess of love, joy, and **prosperity** into the home. Naveen will eat sweet treats all day. He'll go into the city for a firework show once it gets dark. Diwali is the most important holiday to his Indian American family.

Rangoli are placed near the front door. They help welcome Hindu gods into the home.

CHAPTER 2

In the late 1900s, there was a lot of fighting in India. The conflict was between India and its neighbor Pakistan.

LEARN MORE HERE!

MAP OF INDIA

The British government once controlled the land that is now Pakistan and India. When the British gave up control, they divided the land. India and Pakistan fight over a section of land between them. It is located where the map says "line of control."

Indians were tired of living in a dangerous place. They asked their leaders to make changes.

India faced violence from other nearby countries. These issues made life hard for the people. They often took their anger out on each other. Indian Muslims and Hindus started fighting too. Each side tried to hurt the other.

During this time, Indians also faced **economic** and political difficulties. A run of bad leaders had taken poor care of the country and its people. Indians were scared.

Some Indians started to leave the country. They didn't want to worry about getting hurt or about loved ones dying from violence. The United States was a promising place to move to. It offered the safety of religious freedom.

DID YOU KNOW?

India is expected to overtake China as the most populated country by 2024.

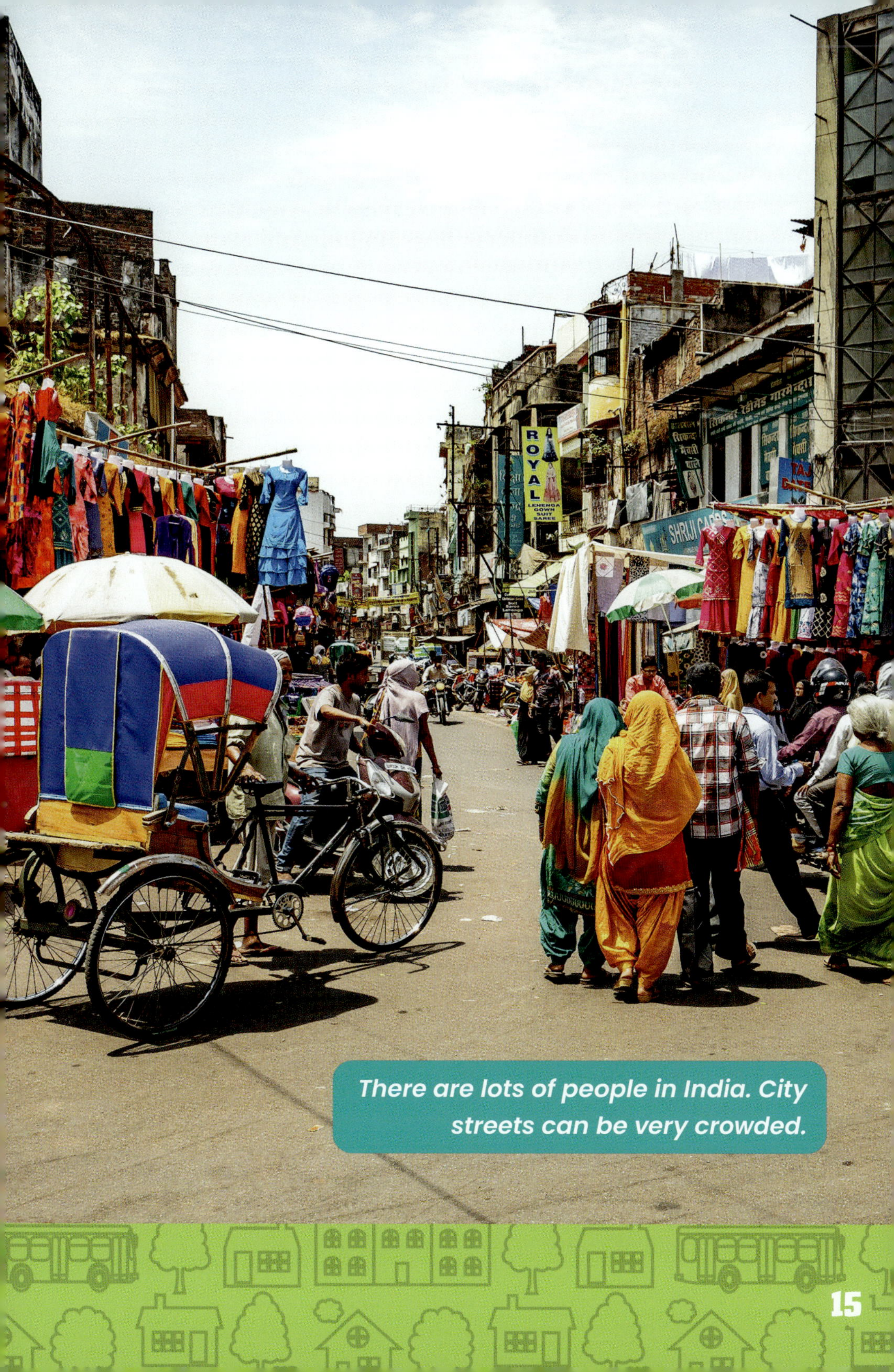

There are lots of people in India. City streets can be very crowded.

HIGH-SKILLED IMMIGRANTS

Indians first started **immigrating** in big groups to the United States in 1968. This was after the Immigration Act of 1965 made the process easier. Americans were strict on whom they allowed into the

COMPLETE AN ACTIVITY HERE!

Indian American students spend a lot of their time studying.

country. They wanted high-skilled workers and people with good educations. The country welcomed immigrants with these qualities. Indian Americans have become the most highly educated and highest-earning group in the United States.

Students can be excited to learn science from teachers as well as from their parents.

Indian Americans came to America looking for a better life for their families. The drive to succeed is common in their households. They take education very

seriously. Children are taught to do their best in school, just like most Americans.

Many Indian American parents work in science, technology, engineering and mathematics (STEM) fields. Their kids are likely to take a similar career path. They may work very hard in science and math classes. They might also join after-school activities that involve **coding** skills.

DID YOU KNOW?

California has the largest group of Indian Americans in the United States.

INDIAN IMMIGRATION TIMELINE

1907-1917

The first small wave of Indian **immigrants** comes to the US looking for better wages.

1947

British rule over India ends.

1919

Famous peace leader Mahatma Gandhi starts calling for an end to British rule.

1948

The war with Pakistan over territory continues throughout the late 1900s.

1968

Indians are officially allowed to immigrate to the United States.

2000s

High-skilled Indians make the move to the United States.

1970s

India experiences war, **economic** trouble, and bad rulers. More people begin wanting to leave.

A BLEND OF CULTURES

Indians brought along a beautiful **culture** when they started **immigrating** to the United States. Before their arrival, Eastern religions were not common in America. India is home to the largest

LEARN MORE HERE!

group of Hindus in the world. Hinduism is a religion that believes there is power in selflessness and learning.

The dot that some Indian women wear in the center of their forehead is called a **bindi.**

Bollywood actors can become as famous as America's Hollywood actors.

Indian culture is now a part of life in the United States. Yoga and meditation came from India. Many forms of mental health care come from Indian **philosophy**. And delicious foods like kebabs and chicken tikka masala were created there.

BOLLYWOOD

Bollywood is part of the Indian film industry. The name is a mix of *Bombay* and *Hollywood*. It is based out of Mumbai (previously called Bombay). All films are in the Hindi language. Bollywood movies often have song and dance numbers. They are full of color and beautiful costumes. Kids like to dance along while watching.

Indian American children sometimes have a hard time understanding where they fit in. They feel close with their Indian background at home. But in school they might not eat the same as their friends. Some Hindus don't eat meat, so their lunches could look different. They also celebrate different holidays than those on the school's schedule.

Indian American families work together to succeed.

DID YOU KNOW?

Indian American Nina Davuluri won Miss America 2014. She was the first winner to have Indian-born parents!

Indian Americans might have different family traditions than their friends. But they also have a lot in common. They go through the same big moments, like riding a bike for the first

Sports are a great way to learn teamwork and grow friendships with people who are different from you.

time, winning a soccer championship, or shopping for back-to-school clothes. Indian Americans are a mix of two cultures. That makes them special and important members of the United States.

MAKING CONNECTIONS

TEXT-TO-SELF

Indian Americans bring Eastern traditions to the United States. Have you ever participated in activities that may be based off Indian traditions?

TEXT-TO-TEXT

Have you read other books about immigrants in America? What do they have in common with this title? How are they different?

TEXT-TO-WORLD

Can you think of any holidays like Diwali where people light lamps or candles? What do they represent?

GLOSSARY

coding — making instructions for a computer.

culture — the arts, beliefs, and ways of life of a group of people.

economic — related to how goods and services are made, sold, and used.

immigrate — to enter another country to live. A person who immigrates is an immigrant.

philosophy — a set of ideas about knowledge and truth.

prosperity — the condition of being successful or thriving.

ritual — an activity with several steps that honors a goddess or god.

symbol — an object or mark that stands for an idea or thing.

INDEX

ONLINE RESOURCES

popbooksonline.com

Scan this code* and others like it while you read, or visit the website below to make this book pop!

popbooksonline.com/indian-americans

*Scanning QR codes requires a web-enabled smart device with a QR code reader app and a camera.